I0158295

Deliverance

Taquayasia's Final Journey

Yasmin Brown

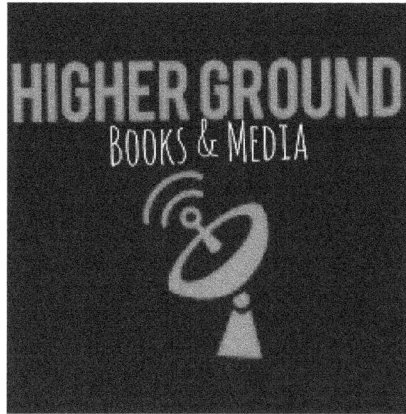

Copyright © 2018, 2019 by Yasmin S. Brown by (Higher Ground Books & Media)
All rights reserved. No part of this publication may be reproduced may be reproduced in any form, stored in a retrieval system, or transmitted in any form, or by any means (electronic, mechanical, photocopying, recording or otherwise) without prior permission by the copyright owner and the publisher of this book.

Scripture taken from the HOLY BIBLE, NEW INTERNATIONAL VERSION®. NIV®. Copyright © 1973, 1978, 1984 by International Bible Society. Used by permission of Zondervan. All rights reserved worldwide.

Higher Ground Books & Media
Springfield, Ohio.
http://highergroundbooksandmedia.com

Printed in the United States of America 2018

Deliverance

Taquayasia's Final Journey

Yasmin Brown

DEDICATION

To all that have been through sexual assault and domestic violence, and who feel like they have lost themselves. For loved ones who supported the survivors in their healing process.

You are not alone in finding your continued strength to heal.

ACKNOWLEDGMENTS

This book is in memory of my grandmother, a domestic violence survivor. On Earth, you were my rock and best friend. In Heaven, you are my angel and spiritual direction. Thank you for allowing me to share the pain and abuse that I went through. You never judged me but supported and love me through it all. With your guidance, I could face it, talk about it, and heal from it. Love you always!

Table of Contents

Chapter One

Unhinged

After Taquayasia left TJ, she felt lost and crushed by what happened. Even though he knew everything she had gone through as a child, he still hurt her mentally and physically. Taquayasia did not feel comfortable talking to her mother or sister about everything she had been through. There was only one person she felt close enough to as a child, her grandmother, Anita. She was a crucial part of Taquayasia's life when she was younger, then later as an adult.

When Anita fell terminally ill with dementia, it was Taquayasia who would help in her medical care over time. No matter how many times Anita would repeat herself in a conversation Taquayasia still loved talking to her. In the weeks that followed, Dementia tightened it's grip on Anita to where they could no longer hold a conversation. This did not stop Taquayasia from talking affectionately with her. During one of Taquayasia's visits, they were talking, and Anita stated randomly, "He will be back." Taquayasia was unclear what she meant but those words stuck with her. When Anita became unable to communicate verbally, Taquayasia felt her world turned upside-down. During another one of Taquayasia's visits to check on Anita, she heard her last words utter to her: "He will be back." Unbeknownst to Taquayasia the impact those words would have on her future.

Three months had gone by when Taquayasia received a devastating call from her father; you grandmother has passed. After Anita passed away her last words to Taquayasia stuck with her. Since she was emotionally sensitive now, everything reminded her of Anita. After crying for a week straight, Taquayasia felt alone with no one to converse with about losing her grandmother or even the things she endured throughout her childhood and her young adult years. At least no one to talk to without feeling their judgment. Losing such an important person in her life made the pain of her past and present that much more real. Missing Anita's love started her back down the road of depression. Feeling her friends and family would be judgmental Taquayasia started to isolate herself. She started staying in the house, dwelling on the fact that the person she could always speak blatantly with was gone.

Caring for Anita, during her years with dementia, was never a problem for Taquayasia. She longed to hear her voice again, even if it was one of the repetitive statements, that often happened at the end. On days that Anita was well enough to get around, she would help Taquayasia take the baby to school. Taquayasia cherished those memories.

Though she felt the pain colliding in her head, she hid it well from others. No one could tell that she was beginning to have suicidal thoughts once again. She was feeling unloved but when she remembered Anita's last words, "He will be back," it stopped her from doing something she could not take back. She spent days thinking about those words and their meaning. She wondered who will be back and what are they coming back to do. She made it her business to seek the meaning of Anita's last words. Does she mean my ex-boyfriends? That was one of the questions that ran through her mind.

Taquayasia started hanging out in bars and clubs from Thursday thru Saturday and sometimes even on Sunday. She wore scandalous clothing trying to catch the attention of her ex-boyfriends. Mentally, her thoughts were all over the place, but on the outside, she kept it together. During one of her nights out, she bumped into TJ, her abusive ex-boyfriend. She was a little nervous to see him but was able to say "Hello." Before TJ walked away, he responded with a head nod.

The next day he called her at 12:00 asking if he can come to see the baby. Thinking he may have changed, she allowed him to come over. While the baby was sleeping TJ was able to sweet talk Taquayasia into having sex with him. As she was lying there with him on top of her, she could not wait until he finished. The next morning TJ waited until the baby woke up before he left. Feeling like she had to walk on eggshells while she was around him started to become too much for her. Not feeling a spark between them, she and TJ sat down to talk about their relationship. They both realized that the feelings were mutual and agreed to go their separate ways but continue to co-parent.

While she was out rejoining the social scene, Taquayasia then ran into Darion. Suppressing the memories of the rape from when they were teenagers, Taquayasia waved at him. Darion strolled over to buy her a drink. After a few cocktails, Taquayasia found herself back in Darion's arms. When she woke up the next morning and noticed Darion next to her, she felt sick to her stomach. Afraid to rock the boat between them she pretended everything was fine. Every time she looked at him, his words would play in her head "I didn't rape you, bitch."

Soon she was drinking to cope with hooking up with Darion, as well as, the loss of her grandmother. Taquayasia felt herself going downhill. She realized that staying with Darion because she was afraid was unhealthy. She knew that she needed to tell him because she was mentally losing control.

A couple of months had gone by since she had last been with Darion and she noticed that she had not gotten her period. Taquayasia decided to take a pregnancy test and picked one up from the store. As she drove home, her thoughts pulled her in different directions, but for the most part, she was not sure if she even wanted to know the results.

At home, after she took the test, waiting for the results felt like a lifetime. But there it was: POSITIVE! The tears started to roll down her face. She knew that she could never give up her child. However, that feeling of having her rapist's baby was devastating. Not ready to face the news, Taquayasia lived in denial and became more unstable. Taquayasia thought of how upset her grandmother would be for her actions. Ring! Taquayasia jumped out of thought as she answered the telephone.

"Hey girl, do you want to go bowling with us?" Months had gone by since she last fraternized outside of Darion. She agreed to go with her cousin to celebrate another family member's birthday. At the bowling alley, she ran into her God-fearing ex-boyfriend from high school. Over a few drinks, they reminisced about when they dated in high school. Taquayasia soon felt that he was the man who would come back into her life. As they finished bowling, Taquayasia announced that she was leaving since it was getting late. She exchanged numbers with her ex, and they agreed to go to an afterhours club sometime.

As she drove home, her cell phone rang. It was her ex-boyfriend from the bowling alley. "Can I come cuddle?" he asked. She agreed to let him over and waited for his arrival. Knock! Knock! Taquayasia opens the door to let him in the house. Closing the door, they headed upstairs to her bedroom. As she lied back in her bed, her clothes still on, her ex-boyfriend sat next to her and put his arm around her. She soon felt relaxed from all her worries. "Can I kiss you?" he asked? She leaned forward and gave him a peck on the lips, then leaned back once more. "Can I have another one?" Before she could respond, he put his big soft lips on hers, placing his tongue in her mouth. They continued to kiss passionately. A short time later their clothes were off and on the floor. After having sex, they both fell asleep for the night. As they woke up in the early morning, he told her that he must leave for church. She felt used and became emotional after acknowledging she was just a booty call for him.

A few days later, she invited him over for breakfast, with the intentions of finding out if he used her. When he arrived, she took him to the kitchen where the bacon, sausage, eggs, grits, and toast was waiting with a cup of orange juice. As they sat across from each other making small talk, she asked casually, "Why are you here?" He responded, "To eat breakfast." She said, "No, why are you back in my life?" Since he was unable to answer the question truthfully, he avoided it altogether. He changed the subject to discussing her relationship with TJ. Seeing that he feared TJ about as much as she did, she gave him a pass on the situation. Once breakfast was over, he tried to get Taquayasia back in bed. But she was turned off by his inability to answer her question and stated that it would not be a good idea. Now aware of his behavior and intentions, she decided to step back from her friendship with him. He tried to persuade Taquayasia by sending her pictures of his genitals. It did not work.

She slowly began shutting herself off from interacting with people and again became anti-social. Staying as active as everyone else became less important to her, moving her into a deeper depression. This caused her to contemplate suicide once again. Her memories stirred flashbacks of being a child at Sunday school. Now looking at things a little differently she started to journal when she felt depressed or down on herself.

On her way to work one morning, she decided to stop for breakfast at a fast food restaurant. While in line, a man approached her and started prophesying over her life to the point Taquayasia started to cry. He ended his speech saying, "I will not remember you or this conversation." Taquayasia left the establishment without ordering any food.

Several weeks later, she was at work and decided to run across the street to the bank, during her lunch break. There she noticed the security guard was the man from the restaurant. She struck up a conversation with him, in hopes of him remembering who she was. However, he merely gave her a 'do I know you' look. She was puzzled by his confusion and left the bank, wondering why he did not know who she was. Returning to work, she let the experience go. Out of sight out, of mind.

As time went on, she forgot all about meeting the man. A week later, while on another lunch break, she took another trip to the bank. As she strolled out, she decided to take a walk while reading a book. She knew that walking and reading was not a good idea, but she did it so often that she was pretty good at it. She devoured books to keep up her knowledge and to give her a peace of mind. Walking past a small park, she had a feeling that she needed to stop there for a break. Taquayasia ignored her instincts and continued to walk a little more. Then the gut feeling to stop for a break grew stronger, so she found a chair in the park to sit down. After continuing to read for ten minutes, she got up and continued on her journey. She did not want to be late getting back to work.

She was almost back to work when she noticed there were fire trucks, police cars, and ambulances crowding the street in front of the building. A car jumped the curb, plowing into a crowd of people before crashing into a brick wall. Taquayasia grew anxious as she got closer, realizing that if she would have kept walking she would have been a part of that crowd struck by the car.

Going back to work, she began to shake as the thought deepened at how things could have turned out if she did not listen to her inner-self telling her to sit in the park. Taquayasia started to cry as she explained the details of the divine intervention to her friend. Now comfortable enough with her friend she also told her about her past and the baby. Taquayasia's co-worker asked her what she was going to do.

That same night she went into labor. Taquayasia called her sister for a ride to the hospital, and once there she told her it was okay for her to go home. She wanted to be alone as she delivered the baby. In fact, she did not even tell anyone until the next morning. As she lied, half asleep in her hospital bed, she tried to figure out what to do with the rest of her life.

Chapter Two

Faith

Taquayasia recalled what led up to her return to church. Feeling mentally lost in so many ways after being molested, date raped and physically & mentally abused. Still feeling that she had no one to talk to, so she decided to attend church. When she woke up that Sunday morning, she felt a heaviness from her depression. Still, she put on a happy face and left for church. Her mother agreed to watch her children. As she drove down the road to church, she was feeling so apprehensive about what to expect that she felt a bundle of nerves in the pit of her stomach. She thought everyone in the church would know her story just by looking at her. She hesitated but proceeded forward to attend. She was still in fear but continued to approach the church doors. When she walked in, she noticed her grandmother sitting in the middle pew and found a seat next to her. As praise and worship carried on, she started to feel fulfilled.

At the end of service, the pastor called for the congregation to receive prayer. Taquayasia decided to go up for prayer. She thought it was what she needed after all of the mental and physical beat downs she had gone through over time. During her walk to the center aisle of the church, she started to feel butterflies in her stomach. When she reached the Pastor for prayer, he laid his hand on her forehead and began to pray. As the pastor prayed, Taquayasia felt so overcome by the Holy Ghost that she fainted. When she woke up, she was lying on the floor, feeling confused. The Co-Pastor helped her up and took her to the side. He then walked her through prayer to receive Christ as her Lord and Savior.

Now that she was saved Taquayasia thought her life was going to change instantly, but that was not the case. Her grandmother has since passed away. Though she continued to attend church, she continues to play those words, "He will be back," every day.

Though mentally disoriented regarding her own life, she found solace in joining church ministries and in reading the Bible.

Her faith helped her to view life a little differently. She was starting to understand that she was still a work in progress with all of her life changes. As she embraced her new values and developed a fresh approach to life, Taquayasia began to serve as an usher, assist with communion, and the praise & worship.

One Sunday morning she was heading to the restroom, and as she walked by the youth class, Mrs. Ann called out to her for help in interpreting the scripture. She stopped in her travels and sat in the chair across from Mrs. Ann to read over the scripture. After Taquayasia explained the chapter to the Sunday school teacher and the class, she got up and proceeded to the restroom. She then went back upstairs to attend services. Taquayasia did not give any more thought to the assistance that she gave to the Sunday School teacher. Unknowingly, that incident would one day lead to assisting with the youth on a regular basis.

After assisting with the youth for several weeks, Taquayasia was asked to take over as the Youth Pastoral Director. Sadly, Mrs. Ann had fallen terminally ill. Though saddened by the news, she accepted her new role. As the children learned from Taquayasia, she too learned. The more she taught the children, the more she felt fulfilled and started to understand her grandmother's last words, "He will be back." Teaching Sunday school helped Taquayasia to gain forgiveness and self-love. Learning how to love herself gave her control over the emotional turmoil from her past, including the impact of the wrongdoings of others. The mental state their actions left her in was starting to have less of a grip on her. The mental, physical, and emotional hold of her past was now spiritually filled with love, encouragement, and self-worth. Taquayasia's faith and activity in church helped her to answer the question of her grandmother's last words.

She discovered another issue in contrast to her new outlook on life. She noticed she lost her sense of control along the way. She began the process of writing in a journal, as a means of expressing her feelings on paper. She believed it would help her to regain control of her life. Until then she found that a lack of power did not allow her to trust many people in her life. After a month of her thoughts going back and forth in her mind, Taquayasia knew there was one more step to take. She needed to seek counseling. As she took steps to find the help, she continued journaling her feelings and emotions when she would feel down on herself regarding her past.

Yasmin's Journal Entries

May 16, 2014

As my prayers get answered, I start to think to myself what an awesome God I serve, for he has blessed me in so many ways. God has delivered me from my past demons and continues each day to help me fight, for each day I struggle. I fight mental demons when my mind starts to race in thought. All the negative energy flowing through my mind when reality hits when I lose sight of my faith. I try to tell myself God is working everything out for my good. It works sometimes, but then something happens to me, and the mental demons are back. I can't shake it away. It's stealing my happiness and peace. I am not worthy of a blessing. Don't give up, fight a good fight in this season. I flip-flop in and out of depression with no one to talk to. I remember I can talk to God. God is still on the throne. God is my provider. Flip-Flop, no one to physically talk to. Flesh cannot help you, only the man that gives me the breath of life each day can allow me to spread my wings.

ⓖَ۫-۬-ۜ—ⓖَ۫-۬-ۜ—...ⓖَ۫-۬-ۜ—ⓖَ۫-۬-ۜ—

May 17, 2015

In a mood, today, feeling emotional detached, flesh and spirit. I am trying to stay focused to remember God is the center holding me together. All I need is just a little more Jesus to help me along the way. God's not through with me yet. Keep your head to the sky. So alone with no one to share my feelings with. Jesus is always there and ready to talk. So many people have done me wrong and don't look back to say I'm sorry, thanks for looking out for me or just say, "Hey how are you doing?" Instead, there are knives, whispers, and stares in my back. No peace, no success, no friends, or family. I try to clear my head before bed. Feeling so fat and out of shape. I want to exercise, but life is so draining I just want to sleep. Peace be still, God said, and I must obey.

ﺍﺧﻔﻔﻔ—ﺍﺧﻔﻔﻔ—...ﺍﺧﻔﻔﻔ—ﺍﺧﻔﻔﻔ

August 12, 2016

I feel I support everyone no matter what their hopes and dreams are in life. All I ever wanted was the same support in return. No one really cares about me unless it benefits them. When I ask someone for help, it's a big deal, or they just don't want to help me. I feel I get more support from strangers than my family. I don't understand what I did for people to dislike me or not believe in me. There is one support system that never changes and is always there - my Lord and Savior Jesus Christ, who will never leave me nor forsake me.

Hang in there Jesus got your back!

ﺍﺧﻔﻔﻔ—ﺍﺧﻔﻔﻔ—...ﺍﺧﻔﻔﻔ—ﺍﺧﻔﻔﻔ

November 24, 2017

As darkness falls on me, I sadden and weep. As my light burns inside me, I just can't reach the Lord that is trying to save me. Lord help me, to find a way to speak, not causing me sadness, remove the shiver and quiver to my voice please allow the rage within me to be released and find peace. Lord turn my frown upside down. Help my light to be reignited through you and remove the pain. Please help me with things I cannot change and work through them with your strength.

Things will get better!

Chapter Three

Counseling

Journaling seemed to be a great help for Taquayasia, but she needed more than that. Even though Taquayasia felt she had a bright future, her past kept revealing itself mentally. Still holding on to hope and faith she decided counseling would be the best way to help her now. She could develop techniques to overcome the thoughts that sent her state of mind into a depression, which lasted longer each time.

Deciding to call the doctor was not an easy task for Taquayasia because she was afraid of what people might say about her. It was even scarier now since she felt obligated to go to the appointment. A few weeks had gone by since she made the call. She was relaxing at home when the telephone rang.

"Hello, may I speak with Taquayasia?"

"Speaking."

"This is Dr. April's office, calling to confirm your appointment for December 9, 2017."

The first appointment was fast approaching, and Taquayasia started to get nervous about her upcoming visit. Before he knew it, the day had arrived - appointment day! Driving down the road feeling nervous and anxious about opening up to a stranger became the scariest thing for Taquayasia. The darkest places of her life were about to be exposed. She started to feel short of breath. Her heart started racing, and within seconds she had a headache. She approached the waiting room and check-in with the receptionist, all the while thinking, 'I can't wait until this is over.' She did not have to wait long for the therapist to call her name. Taquayasia took a few deep breaths and proceeded to the back with the therapist.

When the visit was over, Taquayasia left, still carrying the pain of a headache, but also thinking that seeking help was a great decision to help get back her life. Upon the second visit,

Taquayasia was as nervous as she was for the first session. She left that visit with a foggy head from the suppressed emotions of her past that the therapist stirred up.

Taquayasia decided to go to the gym to work out and release some of the stress she felt. Mentally feeling she was in a better place, Taquayasia left the gym to go to her mother's house to pick up the baby.

Taquayasia scheduled the next visit for the following Saturday, giving her time to recover from that last visit mentally. 'Saturday is here, but the nerves are not' Taquayasia thought. As she walked in the back with the therapist, she felt more at ease about the session. Taquayasia sat in the chair and got comfortable.

"What is new?" asked the therapist. Taquayasia started telling her about her weekend. Everything was going well until the therapist, April, began to ask more probing questions. Taquayasia explained why she was holding onto her past. It was out of fear of not knowing what was ahead of her that drove her to hold onto the unhealthy people and things that harmed her. She spilled out the details of holding on to the pain of being molested and raped, then attempting suicide, It was all too much for Taquayasia as tears started to flow from her eyes. She still feared that TJ might one day kill her, and confronting Darion about raping her made her quiver. Standing on faith Taquayasia faced it all. As the session came to an end, she felt nauseous. Wiping the tears from her eyes, she proceeded to her car.

A week had gone by before the next visit. Taquayasia walked into the therapist's office and took a seat. She was feeling cleansed but did not want to talk about the rape or abuse. This visit was different. April started by saying, "Tell me about your relationship with your family." As she described her family and the roles each member had, she noticed how everyone else had control of her life except her. She left that visit with a task to find ways to take back control of her life in small ways. This included saying "no," and telling other family members that she loved them.

Taquayasia was feeling good about the steps she was taking to regain control of her life. It was then that she decided to write her story. This could be a way to help others who may have gone through similar situations. She thought an interactive self-help book would be a great way to tell her journey. As Taquayasia started to write her book, she found it harder than she thought to tell her story in such intense detail. With each stroke of the pen, she relived every touch of abuse, physical and sexual. She increasingly grew angry and full of tears and resentment for every person who hurt her.

Taquayasia decided to take a break from writing because it became too overwhelming. Some time had gone by which allowed Taquayasia to find herself once again. Finding herself this time gave her the strength to complete the story and dream on a bigger scale for life. Since she had success in healing through creativity, prayer, and therapy, it gave her a great idea to help others through that same creativity.

Continuing with therapy helped her realize that the depth of control that others had over her since she was a child led up to some of the choices she made as an adult. Taquayasia achieved this breakthrough by experiencing the break down that drove her to build her life back up and be strong enough to let go of the past. Now that she is no longer afraid to take control of her life, Taquayasia is ready to take her future by storm.

Chapter Four

Let's Talk

How did you encourage yourself today?

_____
_____
_____
_____
_____
_____
_____
_____
_____
_____
_____
_____
_____
_____
_____
_____
_____
_____
_____
_____
_____
_____
_____
_____
_____

How did you express self-love today?

_____
_____

_____
_____
_____
_____
_____
_____
_____
_____
_____
_____
_____
_____
_____
_____
_____
_____
_____
_____
_____
_____
_____
_____

How did you find inspiration today?

_____
_____
_____
_____
_____
_____
_____
_____
_____
_____
_____
_____
_____

_____
_____
_____
_____
_____
_____
_____
_____
_____
_____
_____
_____

How did you motivate yourself today?

_____
_____
_____
_____
_____
_____
_____
_____
_____
_____
_____
_____
_____
_____
_____
_____
_____
_____
_____
_____

How did you reward yourself today?

_____
_____
_____
_____
_____
_____
_____
_____
_____
_____
_____
_____
_____
_____
_____
_____
_____
_____
_____
_____
_____
_____

How can you take a negative and change it to a positive?

_____
_____
_____
_____
_____
_____
_____
_____

_____
_____
_____
_____
_____
_____
_____
_____
_____
_____
_____
_____
_____
_____
_____

What steps can you take to become my best self?

_____
_____
_____
_____
_____
_____
_____
_____
_____
_____
_____
_____
_____
_____
_____
_____
_____

Encouragement

Fire

As the flame inside me starts to die I sit and wonder why? I cry, Jesus where are you, Jesus where are you! Is it true you will never leave me nor foresake me? Deliver me from this tragedy, build my fire, I want to go higher, I am down on bending knees, please! Jesus can't you see, I cry! I cry, deliver me from this empty place. I am lost in this dark space.

Psalms 18:16-20 KJV

16. He sent from above, he took me, he drew me out of many waters. 17. He delivered me from my strong enemy, and from them which hated me: for they were too strong for me. 18. They prevented me in the day of my calamity: but the Lord was my stray. 19. He brought me forth also into a large place; he delivered me, because he delighted in me. 20. The Lord rewarded me according to my righteousness; according to the cleanness of my hands hath he recompensed me.

About the Author

Yasmin Brown was born in 1977, in McKeesport, Pennsylvania to African American parents. She graduated from college in 1998 and received a second college degree in 2005. She took her degrees and entered into corporate America.

As a survivor of sexual assault and domestic violence, she knew that she was broken but not damaged beyond repair. For years the trauma of her past haunted her. When the memories were triggered, she felt an ache that no one could heal. It was after walking through those dark years that she made the decision to turn to God to rescue her – from herself. His love and guidance wiped the dust away from her heart so that she could love again, especially herself. That breakthrough gave her the strength that she needed to seek help in therapy. When she recognized that so many others were traveling that same lonely path that led from abuse and shame, she gathered her new-found strength and penned her first book, The Silent Destruction, in February 2018. She hoped the book would serve as a guide to help others who are also lost in a state of sadness from pain and betrayal.

With the success of finishing her first book, she went on to write Deliverance. Yasmin did not want just to tell her story but teach it in a way to help someone else turn the corner in their healing. As you follow Yasmin's story, you feel the strength and conviction of the strong woman that she is today. She hopes that with the knowledge and understanding of domestic violence you can find the power and encouragement to help a survivor who is also waiting for someone to bring them their own Deliverance.

Contact the Author:

amazon.com/author/yasminbrown

yazlibra3@hotmail.com

Follow Yasmin on Social Media:

Twitter @yazlibra3

facebook.com/yiryelements

Other titles from Higher Ground Books & Media:

Wise Up to Rise Up by Rebecca Benston

A Path to Shalom by Steen Burke

Overcomer by Forrest Henslee

Miracles: I Love Them by Forest Godin

32 Days with Christ's Passion by Mark Etter

Knowing Affliction and Doing Recovery by John Baldasare

Out of Darkness by Stephen Bowman

The Magic Egg by Linda Phillipson

The Tin Can Gang by Chuck David

Whobert the Owl by Mya C. Benston

Add these titles to your collection today!

http://highergroundbooksandmedia.com

www.ingramcontent.com/pod-product-compliance
Lightning Source LLC
Chambersburg PA
CBHW021922040426
42448CB00007B/877